A catalogue record for this book is available from the British Library

Published by Ladybird Books Ltd Loughborough Leicestershire UK
Ladybird Books Ltd is a subsidiary of the Penguin Group of companies
© Val Biro MCMXCVI
The author/artist has asserted his moral rights
LADYBIRD and the device of a Ladybird are trademarks of Ladybird Books Ltd

Bears Can't Fly

by Val Biro

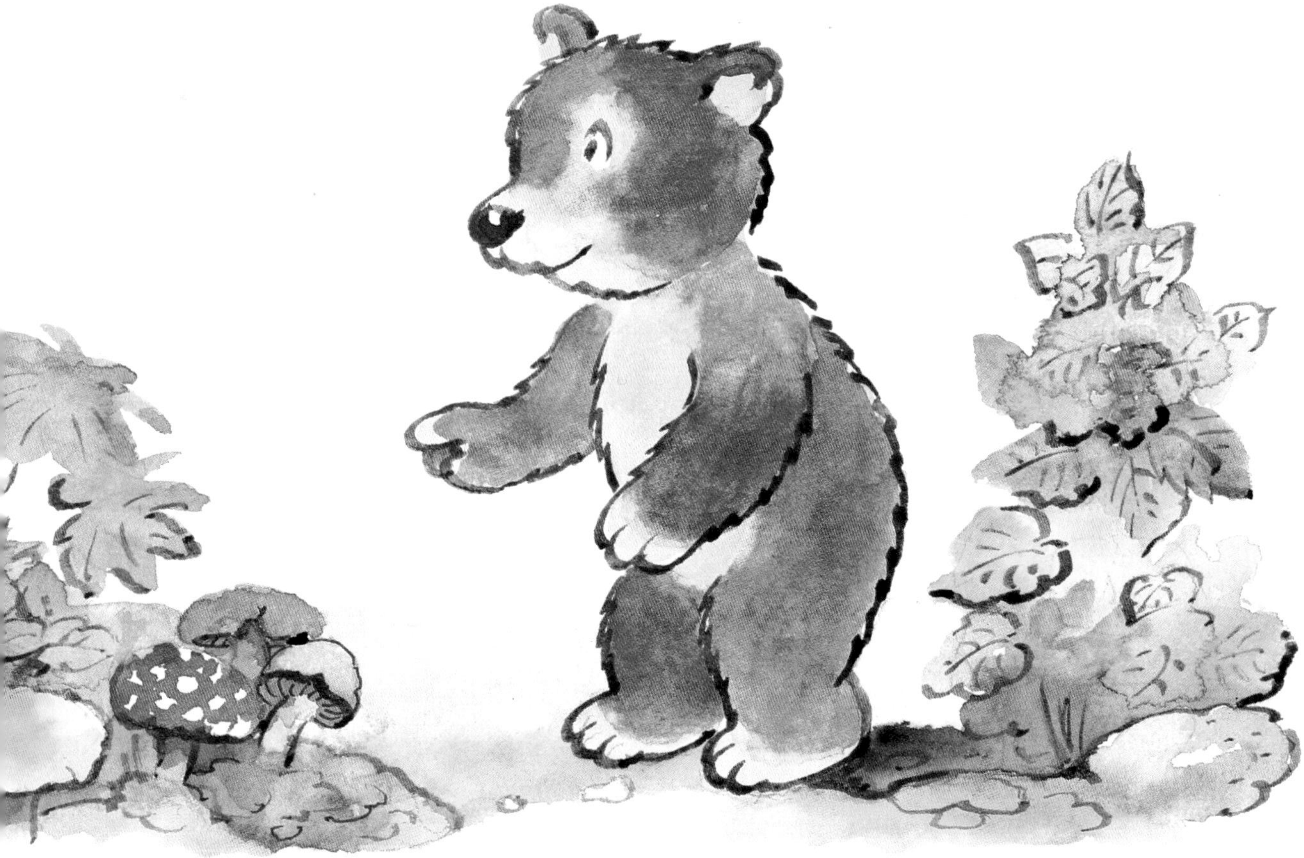

Picture Ladybird

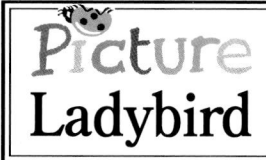

Little Brown Bear lay on his back after breakfast one day and looked up into the forest trees. He saw the birds flying overhead and heard their wonderful songs.

"Now wouldn't it be lovely," he thought, "to fly about and sing all day. Being a brown bear is boring—all I can do is stay on the ground and growl. I'd like to be a bird."

So he hurried through the forest to tell the birds. On his way he swam across a stream and almost stopped to catch a fish for lunch.

But right then he had more important things to do. When he reached the bank, Little Brown Bear shook himself dry. Soon he came to where the birds lived.

"Can you tell me how to be a bird?"
he asked them.

The birds thought this was so funny that they
laughed until they nearly fell out of the tree.

"You can't be a bird," said Owl, "because bears
can't fly. Anyway, you don't have any *wings*."

Little Brown Bear was sad when he heard that, but then he had an idea. He set off for the edge of the forest where the odd-job man lived and explained to him that he needed some wings so he could be a bird.

"Well, I never!" exclaimed the odd-job man. But he didn't laugh because he was kind.

Instead, he set about making some wings out of paper, like two kites, and stuck them on Little Brown Bear's back with sticky tape.

When Little Brown Bear came to the stream again, he did not swim across in case his wings came off. Instead, he fetched a tree trunk in his strong paws and made a bridge.

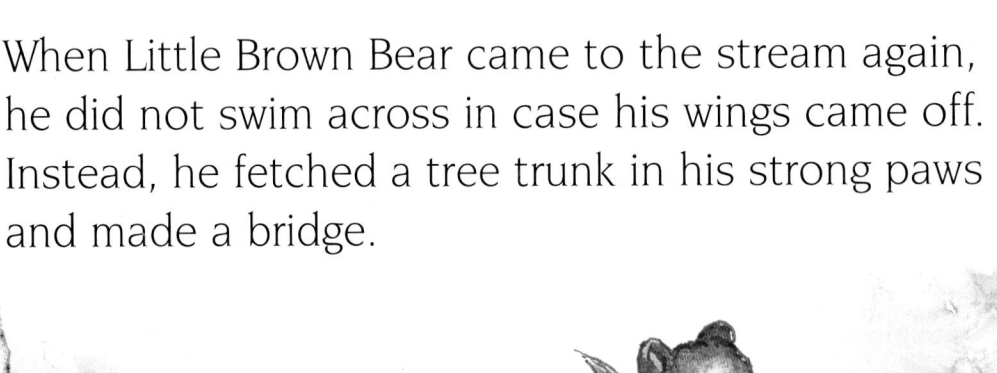

So he walked across the stream without getting wet and continued on to the birds.

"I'm a bird now," he said proudly.
"Look, I've got wings!"

The birds started to laugh louder still, but Owl
stopped them with a look.

"You can't be a bird," he said, "because bears
can't fly. Anyway, you don't have any *feathers*!"

Little Brown Bear was very sad to hear that, but he had another idea. He went to the other edge of the forest where the tailor lived.

"I need some feathers, please," Little Brown Bear told him, "so I can be a bird."

"Fancy that!" said the tailor, but he didn't laugh at Little Brown Bear either.

Instead, he made a coat out of some spare hat feathers and buttoned Little Brown Bear into it. It was only when Little Brown Bear had left that the tailor burst out laughing, and he laughed so much that he had to lie down.

"I'm a bird now!" cried Little Brown Bear to the birds. "Look! I've got feathers!"

Owl shook his head. "You haven't got a *beak*!" he hooted.

"Where's your beak? Where's your beak?" screeched some naughty crows.

"Oh, bother!" said Little
Brown Bear to himself.
"Where can I get a beak?"
Being a bird was very
hard work.

Then Little Brown Bear
had another idea.

"I'll *make* a beak for myself!"
he announced, and dashed
off until he came to a tall
tree. He quickly climbed to
the top and broke off a
piece of hollow branch. With
his sharp teeth and long
tongue he soon turned it into
the shape of a beak – and
stuck the beak on his nose.

There was a puddle on the
ground nearby and when he
saw his reflection in the water
Little Brown Bear thought
that he really looked like
a bird now.

He was in a hurry to show the birds, so he got down on all fours and ran as fast as he could, kite-wings, feather-coat, wooden beak and all.

"Book! Book!" he shouted as he came near. "I'be god a beak! I'b a bird ad last!" He couldn't talk very well with the beak on his nose.

Owl had trouble keeping a straight face.
"Aah, hem. That may be," he said, trying not to
laugh. "But tell me this. CAN YOU FLY?"

Little Brown Bear was indignant.
"Fly? Ob course I cad fly. Book!"

First, he lifted his front paws
and hopped about.

But that wasn't flying.

Then he stood upside down
and kicked his legs
in the air.

"That's not flying, either!"
hooted Owl.

"Bery bell, den," said Little
Brown Bear, "book at dis!"

He climbed to the top of a nearby rock, spread his arms, took a deep breath, shut his eyes and before Owl could stop him… jumped.

Poor Little Brown Bear fell with a THUMP in a pile of leaves and rolled over and over to the great alarm of Owl and the other birds who were watching.

When he got to his feet, Little Brown Bear's beak fell off and he looked a mess. Some of the baby birds couldn't help giggling.

"I told you before," said Owl sternly, "and I'm telling you again, *bears can't fly*. You are a *bear* and bears aren't *meant* to be birds!"

"Wait! Wait!" shouted Bear, determined not to give up. "You haven't heard me *sing* yet!"

And he began to sing in what he thought was the voice of a nightingale.

To tell the truth, it sounded just like the voice of a bear.

A *large*, *fierce* bear.

GROWL,
GROUUWLL,
GROUUUWLLL.

The birds all panicked and flew away as fast as they could. Even Owl took off in a hurry, scattering feathers as he went.

Just then Little Black Bear came toddling by.

"Good afternoon," he said. "What are you growling about here all by yourself?"

When Little Brown Bear told him how he had wanted to be a bird, Little Black Bear smiled. "I know the feeling," he said. "I wanted to be a fish at one time. But I soon realised that being a bear was better. Anyway," he added, "bears can't fly!"

Little Brown Bear sat down to think about this.
After all, many birds can't swim or catch fish.
They can't carry tree trunks or build bridges,
and they certainly had no teeth or long tongues.
What's more, they can't run on two legs nearly as
fast as he can on all fours.

"Perhaps being a bear is not so bad after all," he
said to his new friend.

"Best of all," said Little Black Bear, "birds don't live in warm, snug dens like we bears do. Tell you what, why don't you come back to my den? There's honey for tea."

"Oh, yes please!" cried Little Brown Bear and jumped to his feet. He took off his tattered feather-coat and threw away his ridiculous wings.

"Flying and singing are all very well, but being a bear –" he said, thinking about the honey, "is much, much, MUCH better!"

Picture Ladybird

Books for reading aloud with 2 – 6 year olds

The exciting *Picture Ladybird* series includes a wide range of animal stories, funny rhymes, and real life adventures that are perfect to read aloud and share at storytime or bedtime.

A whole library of beautiful books for you to collect

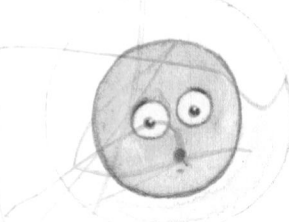

RHYMING STORIES
Easy to follow and great for joining in!

Jasper's Jungle Journey, Val Biro
Shoo Fly, Shoo! Brian Moses
Ten Tall Giraffes, Brian Moses
In Comes the Tide, Valerie King
Toot! Learns to Fly,
Geraldine Taylor & Jill Harker
Who Am I? Judith Nicholls
Fly Eagle, Fly! Jan Pollard

IMAGINATIVE TALES
Mysterious and magical, or just a little shivery

The Star that Fell, Karen Hayles
Wishing Moon, Lesley Harker
Don't Worry William, Christine Morton
This Way Little Badger, Phil McMylor
The Giant Walks, Judith Nicholls
Kelly and the Mermaid, Karen King

FUNNY STORIES
Make storytime good fun!

Benedict Goes to the Beach, Chris Demarest
Bella and Gertie, Geraldine Taylor
Edward Goes Exploring, David Pace
Telephone Ted, Joan Stimson
Top Shelf Ted, Joan Stimson
Helpful Henry, Shen Roddie
What's Wrong with Bertie? Tony Bradman
Bears Can't Fly, Val Biro
Finnigan's Flap, Joan Stimson

REAL LIFE ADVENTURE
Situations to explore and discover

Joe and the Farm Goose,
Geraldine Taylor & Jill Harker
Going to Playgroup,
Geraldine Taylor & Jill Harker
The Great Rabbit Race, Geraldine Taylor
Pushchair Polly, Tony Bradman

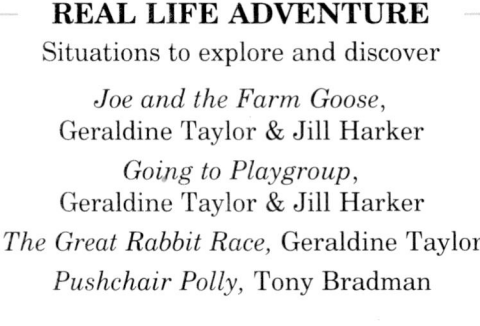